Inquiry

QUOTES & THOUGHTS
BY JIM HICKS

All interior photos by Donnette Hicks **sagecreekequestrian.com** and Kim Stone **shinanatu.com.**

Layout and Design by Emily Kitching.

Published by Eclectic Horseman Communications, Inc.

www.eclectic-horseman.com

TABLE OF CONTENTS

FOREWORD

Kismet is how I first brushed paths with Jim Hicks.

A little over five years ago I had been invited to observe a dressage lesson at Sage Creek Equestrian facility. While there I caught sight of a Mustang in ground training. What I witnessed completely captivated me; I remember thinking to myself, "This is what true horsemanship looks like," and "How is this person communicating with the horse?" At the time I had no idea who Jim Hicks was nor was I familiar with terms like feel or timing in horsemanship. I also had no idea I would soon have a six-month-old weanling of my own.

Sempada, which translates as Blessing, came into my life not long after my visit to Sage Creek. I was as green as they come and quickly realized I was going to need expert training for both of us. I wanted for my young horse what I saw happening for the young Mustang I had observed. So, two and a half years later, off we went to Sage Creek!

We have been working together with Jim for a year and what I have learned about the human-equine relationship has profoundly changed me. Through Jim's patient instruction and hands on work, I have started learning how to use feel and timing as my communication tools. My mistakes are never judged; rather, looked upon as opportunities to learn what works and what doesn't. "An opportunity to clean things up," as Jim tells me. Each day is a new day to check in with the things we know and learn something new in our journey together. The first time

Sempada hooked on with me while at liberty as Jim talked us through an exercise was like capturing magic in a bottle. I stood beside her in the round pen with tears of joy realizing Jim was teaching us what I had observed and wondered about years ago.

Thinking back on the day I first saw Jim training, I now know I was really observing true leadership-maybe for the first time in my life. Jim often reminds me to "Be effective. No more, no less." When I am doubting myself, he will ask reassuringly "were you effective?" Through feel, timing and effectiveness, Jim has been giving me the gift of leadership-with deep respect, gratitude, and a bucket full of joy!

—Kath Christiansen & Sempada

INTRODUCTION

This book serves as a wonderful opportunity to dive into the deep inquiry between humans and their equine companions. It beautifully explores the intricate connections, emotions, and understanding that define our relationships with horses, encouraging readers to reflect on their own experiences while fostering a greater appreciation for the bond shared between humans and equines.

Jim emphasizes that horses often reflect what we project onto them, which encourages us to cultivate mindfulness in every interaction. By considering their needs, we strive to learn their language, which frequently speaks louder than words. By nurturing this understanding, we can foster a deeper connection that enhances not only our relationship but also our personal growth in the process.

- Donnette Hicks

#1

"The most valuable thing I can offer the horse is mindful stillness."

My experiences have taught me that the pause is where the accelerated learning happens for the horse.

#2

"What is not healed on the inside of the rider will reflect back on the outside of the horse."

I have observed that when the rider wants to label their horse, they are confronted by the honest feedback of the horse. This is often a reflection of what's unresolved in the human.

#3

"The horse has allowed me the space to heal the things inside of me that I did not know were broken."

In my experience, the horse is sensitive to the energy of the human—whether that energy is good, bad, or incomplete. I feel I have sensed what was incomplete and that's where I found things that where broken that I needed to heal. They can instinctively sense our emotions and intentions, making their responses incredibly genuine and authentic.

#4

"The human condition seems to be ego, greed and emotional inconsistency. The horse does not have to forgive our failures. However, when the rider becomes authentic the horse seems to forgive our trespasses."

We think we are here to teach the horse something. I have come to believe that the horse is a much older, wiser soul than we are. They allow us the opportunity to evolve as humans.

#5

"I can stand in a room full of people and experience a deep feeling of emptiness. When I stand in the presence of the horse I feel a sense of contentment."

I have never been very good at small talk. In my attempt to avoid awkward silences, I find it hard to connect and be present in the moment. However, with horses, I discover a different kind of comfort in silence; they create a space that allows me to truly be in the moment.

#6

"The rider must find clarity to reduce confusion for the horse."

During my travels teaching, I find that many people are confused and overwhelmed by information. Often, they simply need someone to ask straightforward questions, such as: "What's your goal?" "Why are you doing what you're doing?" "If it's not working, what will you change?"

#7

"The horse that is reacting is surviving. The horse that responds is attuned to the rider, thinking through the situation while seeking relief."

I dislike the feeling of being in a situation where I need to survive. I value the opportunity to pause, clear my thoughts and emotions while thoughtfully considering my response. It makes perfect sense to extend the same opportunity to the horse.

#8

"The unwillingness to make mistakes will limit your ability to evolve in your horsemanship."

From my experience teaching, I've noticed that people often have preconceived notions about what isn't working. This focus tends to amplify their concerns. When I help them shift their perspective to recognize what is working, the conversation transforms quickly, resulting in improved feel and timing.

#9

"Overflexion of the neck disrupts the horse's ability to balance."

I dislike the feeling of being out of balance and would find it upsetting if someone interfered with my equilibrium. I feel a responsibility to act with integrity toward my horse. My experience has shown that overbending the head and neck can lead the horse into a state of mental frustration and physical discomfort. When the horse is overbent, its hind end cannot engage the thoracic sling, disrupting the flow of energy forward. This hinders the natural cycle of energy within the horse.

#10

"The horse gets ready a lot sooner than the human."

I often hear riders say, "I need to prepare my horse better." However, when I ask them what they are preparing their horse for, their anxiety often becomes evident. Meanwhile, I frequently find that the horse already understands the questions and has the necessary tools to respond.

#11

"I used to fight the body to get the mind. Now, I work with the mind, and the body follows."

Anyone can make a horse anxious. A horse that moves in a state of preservation is merely surviving, often moving with unnecessary tension. Rather than just getting the feet to move, I focus on the horse's attitude while moving their feet. A horse that carries unnecessary tension is unproductive. In contrast, a mentally balanced horse moves with relaxation. By focusing on the mind, the feet will follow.

#12

"When the horse and rider feel safe, the learning environment expands in a magical way."

My dyslexia has been my greatest blessing. I've learned to embrace that I process information differently than others. For me, a safe environment is crucial for effective learning.

#13

"It takes courage and humility to recognize the need to relearn a concept."

Throughout my lifetime, I have acquired a set of tools that I know work. As I pursue education to improve myself, I often need to acknowledge the necessity of letting go of outdated thought processes to make room for more evolved ways of thinking.

#14

"I see riders talk and act as though the horse owes them something. As a rider, you are not entitled to anything. The horse will acknowledge your efforts, good or bad. You are either the solution, or you are the problem."

This speaks to our responsibility to take accountability for what the horse does or does not understand.

#15

"My goal is not to emulate anyone specifically, but to embody a collective body of knowledge. There are countless educators who can share their pearls of wisdom. I gather these pearls and incorporate them into who I am, allowing me to move forward powerfully in the world."

Each person I learn from is a treasure trove of knowledge, helping me define what I want to embrace and what I want to avoid in my practice.

#16

"A beautiful dance between horse and rider is developed through good feel and thoughtful timing."

I believe it is my responsibility to be tactful rather than careful. For me, being overly careful with a horse can be dangerous, as it often leads to holding my breath and disrupts my ability to move in rhythm with the horse. In contrast, being tactful means adjusting my feel and timing to establish a flow of rhythm and relaxation, fostering clarity in our connection.

#17

"The difference between mechanics, feel, and timing is simple. Mechanical riding is about submission; riding with feel and timing is about consent."

I believe there is a fine line between submission and consent. I observe people approaching horses as if they need to force them to comply or overcome a concern. This often breeds resistance and resentment in the horse. Even if they achieve submission, it tends to be short-lived and takes away from the horse's nature. I prefer to approach the horse with respect and clarity, educating myself on their needs. Through good feel and thoughtful timing, I aim to communicate in a way that honors their nature and preserves their dignity.

#18

"Each horse that I work with has a different set of needs. Each requires something unique from me. My job is to figure out what that is."

While I have certain knowledge, I am more intrigued by what I don't know. My curiosity lies in what the horse is willing to teach me.

#19

"Offering a feel that inspires trust will develop the necessary timing that enhances balance. This encourages the horse to move with freedom and ease."

⁓

Riders often think they need to teach horses how to organize their bodies in an athletic manner. Most horses are inherently athletic until we intervene. I frequently hear, "I need to teach my horse to change leads." However, I've observed horses change leads effortlessly on their own. The issue lies not in the horse's ability but in the rider's failure to communicate in a way that makes sense to the horse.

#20

"Comfort and concern, when applied thoughtfully, enhance the horse's ability to regulate emotions."

Does your horse find relief in movement? If your horse feels anxious while moving, why is that? The horse perceives the movement as either a source of comfort, or a source of concern.

#21

"A confused and distracted rider limits their ability to guide the horse with clarity."

A rider who establishes reference points during the ride can create a specific line of travel. This line of travel provides the rider with crucial information on what adjustments to make. It's important to note that I'm not referring to mechanical communication; rather, we need to consider how to adjust the feel and timing of the horse's feet.

#22

"The nature of the horse is different than the nature of the human. As riders we have a responsibility to the horse not to confuse the two."

The nature of the horse is fundamentally different from that of humans. We bear a significant responsibility to recognize and respect these differences, ensuring that our expectations and communication do not blur the lines between our human perspective and the horse's nature. By acknowledging and honoring the inherent differences, we can cultivate an effective partnership.

#23

"The horse has a way of humbling the rider who becomes inconsiderate and/or unfeeling."

When we forget to consider and feel things from the horse's point of view, the horse will not willingly participate.

#24

"*Rhythm is a good indicator of emotional and physical balance.*"

The horse and rider synchronize through feel and timing, establishing a consistency in rhythm.

#25

"The rider that has learned to regulate their energy will not create any unnecessary concern for the horse."

I have observed that many horses become alarmed by human movement. Most people have not learned to recognize the energy they convey to the horse and how it influences the fight or flight response.

#26

"Great horseman don't seem to be overly impressed with what they know."

These individuals continuously educate themselves by considering various perspectives.

#27

"The rider who learns to adjust as many times as necessary will learn to meet the needs of the horse."

Each horse will teach you what you need to know if you are open to observing what works and what doesn't.

#28

"The rider that can learn to see things from the horse's perspective can develop a way of communicating that is understood by the horse."

Understanding a horse's perspective requires patience and empathy, enabling the rider to forge a deeper connection. By recognizing the horse's instinctual nature, the rider can foster cooperation. Ultimately, a rider who can see through the horse's eyes cultivates a rooted partnership.

#29

"The horse's reaction or response is a reflection of the horse's interpretation of the rider's energy."

The horse's reaction often reflects its interpretation of the rider's energy, making it essential to understand the horse's perspective. This insight into the horse's viewpoint is crucial for fostering trust and communication in the partnership.

#30

"The horse is learning what you want or what you don't want with each step. Ride the steps that are useful."

When I am consciously choosing to reward wanted actions and redirecting unwanted ones, I can effectively shape the horse's process.

#31

"I would rather have my horse know one thing really well than be confused about 10 things."

I need to stress the significance of depth rather than re-petitiveness in training, while underlining the belief that a horse can thoroughly master one skill instead of being inundated with several skills.

#32

"When the rider reaches for the reins,

the horse has a couple of choices. They can

brace for impact, or they can soften and feel

back to the rider's hands in preparation to

move through a feel that inspires trust."

For years, I have noticed the following:
- Riders reaching for the reins
- Horses responding to the lack of feel from the rider

The way the horse responds not only influences the immediate ride, but also plays a crucial role in fostering relatedness between the rider and the horse, ultimately enhancing their performance together.

#33

"The sensitivity of the horse is only as good as the feel the rider has to offer."

For me, a horse's innate sensitivity can only be fully realized when the rider possesses a keen sense of feel and awareness. My connection is crucial; a rider who is attuned to the subtle movements of the horse can foster a more empathetic relationship. The depth of the horse's responsiveness is directly linked to the rider's proficiency in conveying their intentions, making a skillful and essential agreement.

#34

"Any skill being introduced can be a source of comfort or a place of anxiety to the horse."

When I am introducing a new skill to a horse, I realize that I can evoke a range of emotions. For some horses, learning a new task presents an opportunity. I also realize that the prospect of a new skill can provoke apprehension, as the horse may feel uncertain or overwhelmed by unfamiliar expectations. This can manifest in various ways, from resistance to a lack of focus.

#35

"The question people ask me consistently: 'Is the horse trainable?' My question to the person is, 'are you willing to adjust as many times as necessary until the horse understands what you are teaching?'"

When people ask me if a horse is trainable, my response tends to shift the focus back to the person—are you prepared to modify your approach as many times as it takes until the horse grasps what's being offered? Ultimately, it is a mutual understanding and effort that paves the way for meaningful progress and connection.

#36

"There is what I think happened. There is what the horse thinks happened. I learned to recognize that the horse's opinion is the one that counts. The horse will teach me how to help support their needs."

I've come to realize that there are two perspectives:
my interpretation of events and the horse's own perception.
By opening up to invaluable insights that guide me in meeting
the horses needs more effectively, the horse becomes the teacher
in the art of understanding.

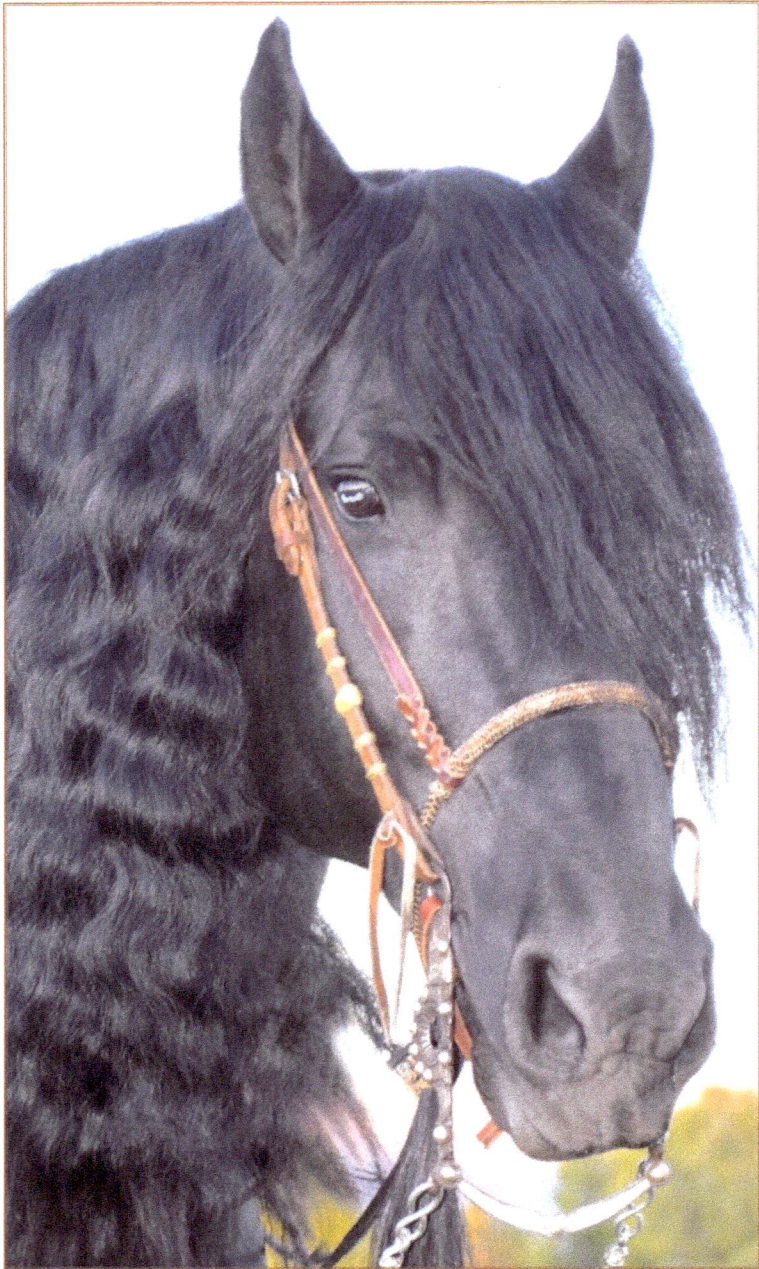

#37

"Riders seem to feel the need to put labels on their horses. They usually tend to be degrading to the horse. My response? Give your horse a reputation that you want them to live into."

Riders often feel compelled to label their horses, but these labels can frequently be limiting and even degrading. Labels like "stubborn" or "lazy" can create a self-fulfilling prophecy, negatively impacting both the horse's behavior and the rider's mindset. My response is to cultivate a more empowering environment for the horse—one that reflects its potential and qualities that one wishes to nurture. Riders can foster an environment that inspires the horse. This shift in perspective not only enhances the relationship between horse and rider, but also opens the door to a more fulfilling and constructive experience.

#38

"If the rider is not willing to offer direction for the horse, the horse will direct the rider."

When the rider does not give the horse enough information, the horse is going to do what horses do. Sometimes they get playful, other times they become fearful. The horse is going to express this in different ways depending on the situation.

#39

"Consistency of communication creates clarity and understanding for the horse."

I strive for consistency in my communication, which is essential for fostering clarity and understanding between myself and the horse I'm working with. Horses perceive their environment through a lens of interactions that can feel either rough or smooth, influencing their responses.

#40

"As the horse develops a higher degree of softness and sensitivity in training, the rider must hold themselves to a higher standard of accountability for the horse."

This means being more attuned to the horse's needs and responses, ensuring that their own actions are clear and consistent. By holding myself to a higher standard, I develop a more respectful partnership, encouraging the horse to not only progress but to also thrive.

#41

"At times, the rider will need to do less to get more. Other times, the rider will need to do more in order to do less."

When I am doing less I am allowing the horse to explore and respond, fostering independence and confidence. There are times when I must increase my effort-whether through clearer communication, or heightening my awareness—to receive more straightforward responses from the horse.

#42

"The words you use to describe your horse can either create a masterpiece or dismantle it. Choose your words wisely."

Horse owners often overlook that focusing on a problem only serves to magnify it. When I encounter a challenge with a horse, I immediately recognize it as an opportunity for mastery.

Our words profoundly influence our lives, directing our approach to every situation. For instance, if someone labels their horse as a "knothead," focusing on that trait will only exacerbate the issue.

When I face difficulties with a horse, I shift my mindset to view it as part of my learning journey. This perspective encourages me to build the horse's confidence and foster admiration. I seek ways to further my horse so that it feels secure rather than defensive. This approach is honest, authentic, and constructive.

The distinction lies in how we often get caught up in rigid systems, methods, and binary thinking, leading to conclusions of "right" and "wrong." Such thinking severely limits what we believe our horses are capable of and can create a dis-empowering mindset.

Instead, I prefer to explore the possibilities of what is working with the horse.

AFTERWORD

My first experiences with horses were rooted in my family. However, I often found my-self in a situations that I shouldn't have been exposed to, leading to negative encounters filled with fear—both for myself and horses. It's interesting I chose a profession involving horses, especially since there was a time when I lacked the confidence I needed. While I was able to get things done, the quality of my work suffered.

I began to hear about a man named Ray Hunt, who discussed concepts like "feel and timing" and "seeing things from the horse's perspective." These ideas resonated with me, while other clinicians left me feeling skeptical.

My first introduction to Ray came when I audited a clinic. As I listened and observed, I witnessed positive changes in the participants and their horses. I recognized capable individuals achieving results, but Ray's approach was unlike anything I had seen before.

While clinic participants focused on their challenges, I became captivated by the dialogue occurring between Ray and his horse amid those challenges. I noticed the subtle adjustments he made, and within about 45 minutes, I had a realization: I wanted to unlearn everything I thought I knew about horses and explore the conversation Ray was sharing. That moment marked the beginning of my passion for working with horses. Now thirty-plus years later Ray's inspiration continues to carry me as I travel and share horse-manship principles across the United States.

- Jim Hicks, October 2025

www.ingramcontent.com/pod-product-compliance
Lightning Source LLC
Chambersburg PA
CBHW041604260326
41914CB00012B/1388